CROP CIRCLES
THE LATEST EVIDENCE

Since the publication of the international bestseller *Circular Evidence*, more and more circles of flattened crops have appeared in the fields of southern England. And not just circles: the formations that were recorded in the summer of 1990 included rectangles, rings, spurs, fingers, beautiful patterns, elaborate hieroglyphs and even a triangle. These unexplained – and apparently inexplicable – configurations are now widely acknowledged to be one of the greatest unsolved mysteries of the twentieth century. Who or what is causing them? Why have they recently been seen so much more frequently and become so much more complex? Read *Crop Circles: The Latest Evidence* and see why this phenomenon has baffled even the experts.

Pat Delgado is a retired electro-mechanical engineer and Colin Andrews is chief electrical engineer with the Test Valley Borough Council. They are founder members of the Circles Phenomenon Research Group.

Pat Delgado & Colin Andrews

CROP CIRCLES
THE LATEST EVIDENCE

BLOOMSBURY

PAT DELGADO

COLIN ANDREWS

First published in Great Britain 1990
Bloomsbury Publishing Limited, 2 Soho Square, London W1V 5DE

Copyright © 1990 by Pat Delgado and Colin Andrews

A CIP catalogue record for this book
is available from the British Library

ISBN 0–7475–0843–7

PHOTO CREDITS

Peter Andrews: page 13
Rick Howell: pages 49, 50, 51 *top*, 61 *top*, 62, 63, 67
Kenneth Spelman: page 42

All other photographs by the authors

Line drawings by Neil Hyslop

Typeset by Bookworm Typesetting, Manchester
Printed by Butler and Tanner Limited, Frome and London

The most beautiful thing we can experience is the mysterious. It is the source of all true art and science.

ALBERT EINSTEIN, 1879-1955

To Wendy, Norah and Jan,
for their continued
help and support.

We would like to thank all the farmers who kindly permitted
us to enter their properties during our research, in
particular John Guy of Chilcomb Farm, Stephen Horton
of Firs Farm and Gerald James of Hazeley Farm.

Contents

*I*NTRODUCTION

Circular Evidence hit the bestseller lists around the world in 1989 and was instrumental in the resulting huge interest from the public, researchers and official bodies in many countries.

This update is the result of the demand for more information about what is now widely acknowledged as the biggest mystery of the century, joining such unresolved subjects as UFOs, poltergeists and spiritualism. In my view a thread may connect them all and an untouchable distant dimension is becoming nearer as our mental consciousness shifts more quickly than at any time in recorded history. One has only to see the global concern so sincerely felt by people everywhere and the political skittles being knocked down and reassembled. We are seeing a planet close to death and yet equally near to rebuilding a society that knows its place in nature.

I am more convinced now than when we finished writing *Circular Evidence* that a conscious process is involved with this most striking symbolism ever produced in our midst – these beautiful patterns have evolved even further and ever more bizarre experiences have been reported.

COLIN ANDREWS
AUGUST 1990

CROP FORMATIONS CHEESEFOOT HEAD, *1989*

We are back at one of the most prolific circle locations, Cheesefoot Head, about two miles southeast of Winchester in Hampshire, the ancient capital of England. I planned the largest surveillance operation of its kind, Operation White Crow, and from 10 to 18 June the latest infra-red and image-intensifier cameras were focused into the natural amphitheatre below and the images recorded on video in vehicles positioned behind the hawthorn hedge on a bank beside the A272 highway. The owner of the field, Commander Bruce, was growing peas, a crop very rarely involved, and would not permit research on his land. This was the best alternative.

Over fifty observers were invited to take part, many of them scientists and engineers. It was uneventful until 3.30 a.m. on the night of 12 to 13 June when several people saw a bright stationary object appear suddenly above and behind the field. It held the same position for four to five minutes. Ron Jones, one of the observers, was adamant he could detect movement from within the orb of the object. A heavy goods vehicle broke the night silence as it climbed the hill from Winchester towards the Punch Bowl. At the moment the lorry's headlights struck out across the field the object disappeared.

I arrived the following morning and the key witnesses, Ron Jones and Terry Clarke, passed to me the videotapes of that shift. But it was some days before all the tapes were checked, because an operation of this size, coinciding with the British launch of *Circular Evidence*, placed extreme pressure on us.

White Crow concluded on the morning of Sunday 18 June with a most strange experience – one that I still think about almost daily. On the Saturday morning the postman made a delivery to my Andover home. I was tired from the gruelling schedule and only intended a quick look at the letters he brought. But one caught my eye – a brown envelope, posted in Rochdale, with 'First Class, Utmost Urgency to Read' above my name and address. And on the reverse of the envelope, 'Very Urgent, Information re White Crow'. I opened it immediately. In grey pencil a child-like hand conveyed a message from an unnamed group. I discussed it with several good friends, who advised me not to publish the confidential contents. Suffice it to say, the message referred in detail to the most weird experience which was to end White Crow.

In the closing hours of White Crow I asked eight colleagues to walk with me along the road, 300 metres to the east and on to the Longwood Estate where a large circle had appeared some days earlier, one of a pair in the same barley field.

We nine sat in this circle not long after midnight and after about ten minutes of complete silence I heard a low-level warbling noise. It was strikingly similar to one I had experienced in frightening circumstances some two years earlier at Kimpton (page 66 of *Circular Evidence*). Looking at the faces nearby I waited for the first indications that they too could hear it. I broke the silence: 'Can you hear what I can hear?' All together they replied, 'Yes.' Pat was alongside me and he seemed much more involved with what was happening, in a funny way almost part of it, as if rehearsed.

I cannot bring it upon myself to describe the fine detail of what happened over the following twenty-five minutes or so. A painful control mechanism in the bottom of my stomach forces the movement of the pen as I write this. The noise came from the fields to the east and became louder as it surrounded us, moving close to Pat and myself. We stood and walked towards it, while the group remained sitting. As the noise backed away from the two of us, having come to within a few feet, it moved back to where it had come from. Pat felt instinctively that we should leave the circle and this we did. It seemed as though we had virtually shaken the hand of an invisible entity. Was it the circle creator? Whatever it was, it was strange in the extreme.

We walked to the surveillance vehicles. One of the observers, George Wingfield, suggested I return with him to the circle with my tape recorder. Five minutes later there we were, and suddenly there 'it' was too. It appeared to be flirting with us but all the time keeping to the east of us. Most importantly I was able to record it. As dawn approached a police car stopped and asked if we were aware of a new dramatic circle and ring in the field to the east. We did not know of this new circle's existence but this was the area to which the noise had moved away. Ten days and nights,

fifty observers and equipment worth £30,000 watching the field to our north, and the new arrival appeared in the field to our east. Bad luck, intelligence or coincidence?

When the White Crow videotapes were eventually played back we were excited to find we had captured the orange ball of light that had appeared on the night of 12 to 13 June. It had not created a circle and was far distant from the field, so what were we to make of it?

A colleague, Professor Archie Roy, viewed the film and was sure it was not the moon or any other planet. We were also certain it was not an aircraft of any kind.

In *Circular Evidence* on page 115 there is another eye-witness account of an orange light coming from above into a field where there were already circles.

COLIN ANDREWS

BECKHAMPTON, 1989

The 'noise' made its first television appearance during a very special day at Beckhampton in 1989. Pat and I were being interviewed by a BBC film crew for *Daytime Live*. I had just completed my interview at 3.00 p.m. on Thursday 10 August and Pat took up his position near the centre of this very large 40-metre circle and ring. We had both experienced great difficulty with our performances and felt a ton weight on top of our heads. I felt as though my tongue was tied to the roof of my mouth and that my lips and brain were not synchronised.

The BBC were using a £50,000 high-tech videocamera, but each time it approached this circle and the smaller ones nearby, it malfunctioned. Noise bars of interference crossed over the recording and red lights flashed indicating all kinds of problems.

As Pat began his interview with a microphone attached to his tie, I stood close to the edge of the circle with the sound technician, Richard Merrick. The producer, David Morganstern, and director, John Macnish, gave the instruction to roll. Richard said at once, 'What is that?' From his headphone came the 'noise' and I could hear it too. It was loud and broke across everything being recorded. At the same time Pat could feel a powerful energy field engulfing him. As he moved out of the immediate area Richard said, 'It's gone.' Pat walked several times over the spot and each time the sound would respond on recording equipment.

The BBC amazed British viewers when they included the full sequence in the programme. The noise was later analysed by BBC sound experts and remains a mystery, as do the serious problems with the camera, which had to be completely rebuilt at great cost. The whole team were affected by the day they investigated the mystery crop circles; they describe what happened in *The Daytime Live Book*.

COLIN ANDREWS

LOCKERIDGE, 1989

Late in the 1989 season for crop circles we received a telephone call from a farmer, Mr Cutforth, whose land is south of the small village of Lockeridge in Wiltshire. He told us there was a large circle surrounded by rings in one of his fields. Colin and I met and drove to the locality full of the usual anticipation and excitement, and Mr Cutforth escorted us to a field on one side of a valley.

From a high position we were able to look across the valley into a field where we could see a very big circle surrounded by narrow rings. In the foreground were other small circles which looked insignificant compared with the diameter of the large one. After taking some photos using a zoom lens, we crossed the valley and excitely walked up the slope of the wheat field and into the huge flattened circle.

We were very impressed with the distance between us and the other side of the circle; it was an immense area to be flattened. Then we turned our attention to the surrounding rings. Strange things had occurred with the creation of these rings, and the gap-seeking factor (the tendency of the energy to be attracted into spaces around the edge) was evident where the rings ran into the tractor-wheel tracks. Confusion had certainly taken place and it was one of the most important details because the gap-seeking element provides a major clue to understanding how the creative energy is operated and how it can be influenced.

Three narrow rings were formed with concentric harmony in the plain crop area. The measurements we took showed the clockwise-swirled circle diameter was 32 metres. The first standing band was 2 metres across. The inner ring was 60 cm wide and flattened anti-clockwise. The second standing band also measured 2 metres. The middle ring was 50 cm wide and flattened clockwise. The third standing band was 1 metre wide and the outside ring was only 10 cm wide and also flattened clockwise. It could be that the middle and outside rings were the two parts of the second ring but tractor-wheel tracks on both sides of the circle had had sufficient influence to split it into two parts; the total of the two widths would have made the second ring the same as the inner ring.

Just for interest, the circle site is close to a very long Roman fortification ditch and ridge named the Wansdyke. In the overall photograph the remains of a Roman settlement can be seen top right as well as the tell-tale tracks made by our car coming down from our first viewing point in the green field on the other

side of the road. The erratic track in the foreground is a feature we have noticed close to many circles. The crop stems in these tracks are only partially flattened and often have dead-end branch lines. Yet another mystery.

PAT DELGADO

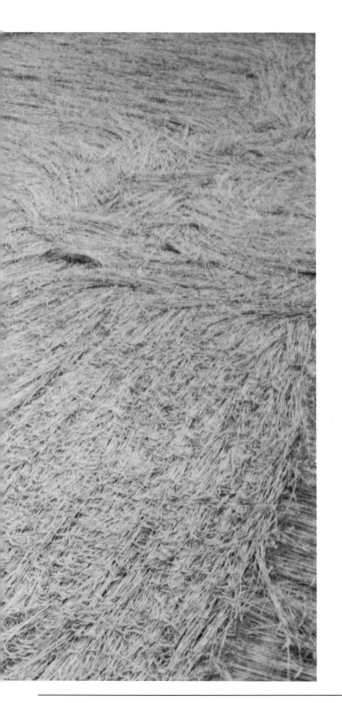

WINTERBOURNE STOKE, 1989

Farmer Mike Bucknell had only ever seen circles once on his land, referred to on page 103 of *Circular Evidence*, but he should not have been surprised when a young student working for him walked open-mouthed into an amazing 21·4-metre-diameter circle. He could not understand what he was looking at and went to report it.

The first person the student met was Peter Molyneux, also a farm employee. Peter had read *Circular Evidence* and had seen the circles in 1987. He went over to have a look and found two other smaller circles, measuring 6 metres and 5·35 metres, only 16 metres away from this large circular picture of beauty. The floor pattern was most striking and one of the most impressive we had seen up to that time. About two miles to the east a single circle had been found just off the western end of the Boscombe Down runway. It had appeared on 10 July, about one month before this latest Winterbourne Stoke event.

In mid-August another amazing circle appeared, about a quarter of a mile west of Winterbourne Stoke along the A303 highway and just out of view of it. It had an 18·5-metre diameter, with a unique pattern of plants flattened into four quadrants and laid at right angles along the four partings. A 1-metre-wide clockwise band lay around the circumference, half of which lay under the heads of surface quadrants.

I thought that these intricate ground patterns looked as if they had been created by a method consisting of a single point of contact, formed as if drawing such a shape with the point of a pen at great speed.

COLIN ANDREWS

CHILCOMB FARM, *1990*

It was mid-June, and one of those rare occasions when I had been unable to drive round my morning observation route. Consequently Bob Trevellyan, a keen crop watcher, telephoned me about a new formation he had spotted while driving to work. His description of the new pattern was almost unbelievable, so as quickly as I could I gathered my equipment together, tried to contact the farmer and drove to the site.

Arriving on the scene I could see this was something completely new. Even the initial oblique roadside view was a breathtaking sight. John Guy, the farmer, who is very interested in this mystery and is always helpful, confirmed it had not been there the previous evening. Tentatively entering this formation I was overcome with a great feeling of wonder and respect and an awareness of special energies pervading the scene. Energy is the key factor to the creation of all crop formations. Over the past few years I have gradually become aware of its existence. Of course, it is quite obvious an energy of some kind is always at work here, but my ability actually to feel and relate to this energy is still escalating. I describe this more fully in the Theories Update section.

As always, the first thing was to sketch the pattern and note the various swirls and straight lie of the crop in the central pathway and rectangular troughs. It was the four troughs that struck me as really special; they had never occurred before. They were entirely remote from the central pathway with no connecting track except for a wisp of two or three crop stems. This wispy feature has now been noted as something common to isolated

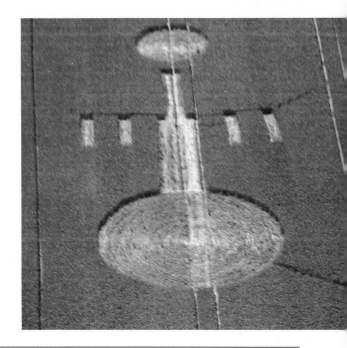

parts of formation patterns, and it reminds me of drawing letters with icing on a cake and the icing occasionally trailing off at the end.

Two strange features were apparent. The shoulder where the central path changed widths was curved downwards from the narrow to the wider part, and the end on the narrow path did not enter the smaller ring. Looking from the larger circle towards the smaller one, the left edge of the wider pathway did not run into the tractor-wheel track but left a thin line of standing crop about 8 cm wide. The left-hand edge of this wide path was not so well defined as the right, as though some strokes that had induced it to lie flat were missing.

One of the most important details was on the floor of each trough. At first it seemed all four were swept away from the large circle end, but closer examination revealed a strip of crop about 24 cm wide flattened in the opposite direction. This contraflow was on the central path side in all four troughs, one pair a mirror image of the other.

The demarcation line between the edge of the large circle and the beginning of the central path was extremely sharp. The crop stems were at right angles to each other with not one stem out of place. This type of

precision also occurred in the troughs where there was a sharp definition at the end from which the stems were swept away. The other end of the trough floor was even more interesting. The drill lines of the crop became divided as they were swept into the standing edge at that end. It gave the impression that a large comb with 10-cm spacings between the teeth had been used.

This was a massive leap forward in displayed phenomena and it was impossible to absorb all the implications at the first visit. We were no longer dealing with only circles and rings and it was important to find a word that gave some idea of what we were looking at. I telephoned the British Museum, thinking 'hieroglyph' might be the word to use, but was informed that this is used in reference to carvings on stones and that the word 'pictogram' would be more appropriate. Hence, from that day onwards every crop formation of intricate design has been termed a 'pictogram'.

Little did Colin and I know at that time what permutations of shapes were to come with the emergence of a phenomenon of unprecedented significance.

PAT DELGADO

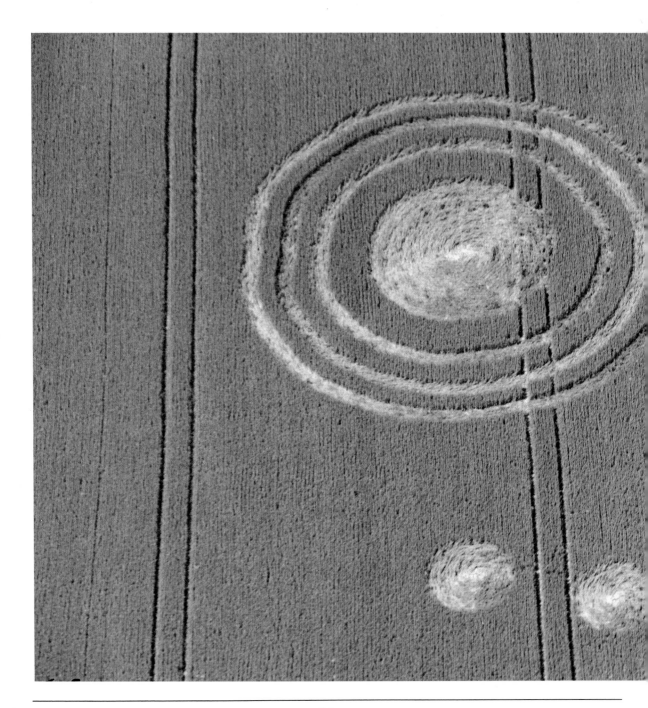

LONGWOOD ESTATE, *1990*

Two striking and complex formations arrived within one week on the Longwood Estate, south of the A272 highway, near Winchester, Hampshire. The most well defined three-ringer was found by Matthew Lawrence, a keen circle spotter, while scouting the area on 30 May. He could see the rings sparkling as the stems, flattened very firmly on the ground, reflected the early morning sun, as if a cosmic artist had painted his artistry with white gloss paint.

You would have thought Matthew had won the football pools after his discovery, but we understood the feelings evoked by one's first find. One does not usually win the pools twice. However, on his regular morning trip around the known circle sites, he could not believe his luck when on 6 June, at about the same time, he saw another marking in the same field. This one was very different. Much closer to the road, it consisted of two split rings and a completed annular ring encompassing the whole.

Pat and I arranged to meet at the circle later that day, and I saw a look of near terror on Pat's face as he went sprawling across the central circle in front of me; a very high level of energy had come upon us. I have watched my colleague and friend become more and

more in tune with the energies at work in these circles and at times have become alarmed at the effect they have upon him. I respect his judgement on this whole area of involvement and leave it to him to disclose what he wishes.

We feel that the time is now right to say a little more about the phenomenon. Those of you who have dabbled with a ouija board will know that communication of another kind can occur. Once you accept that other forms of intelligence are associated with this, then *Circular Evidence* becomes easier to believe. However, I do not recommend that you experiment with a ouija board. The best way into this unknown dimension is through the mystery circles positioned in the fields of southern England.

COLIN ANDREWS

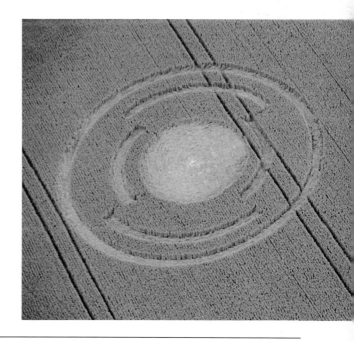

TELEGRAPH HILL, 1990

Once again a report in mid-June from another keen crop watcher, Steve Cole, saw me rushing off to investigate a bizarre formation fairly close to the Chilcomb Farm site.

As I approached from the road I could not determine any definite shapes of the formation because of the oblique view. It was situated halfway up the steep side of Telegraph Hill and only presented what appeared to be a circle with an attached pathway. Full of anticipation and excitement (yes, after all these years it has not diminished) I assembled my camera pole. This, by the way, is a magnificent improvement on my earlier model. It's an ex-TV aerial pole, cut into four lengths each 1·2 metres long and socketed together so that, including my height when I am holding it aloft, the camera is 6·5 metres above the ground.

I entered the field next to the first pictogram and walked up a tractor-wheel track into a swirled circle which was part of an amazing pattern. After soaking in the beauty of this freshly created circle I walked along a pathway that entered a second circle. I noted how sharp the edges were of both circles and pathway.

It was when I entered the second circle I noticed with astonishment three semi-circular

ring pathways partly surrounding it. There were no connecting pathways or tracks into the semi-rings; they were entirely remote from the second circle. Measurements showed these semi-rings and spacings were very regular and concentric. Both circles and the two inner semi-rings were flattened clockwise, while the outer semi-ring was flattened anti-clockwise. The side view in the ground-shot photograph is important because it demonstrates once again the precision with which some of these patterns are formed. This particular configuration seems to be entirely uninfluenced by the direction of the tractor-wheel tracks, an important point when trying to establish common factors for this phenomenon.

While standing in the formation I was able to look down into the Chilcomb Farm pictogram. The impact of the energy surrounding me together with that felt from the formation below – a 'double-sensed' energy – was very apparent.

What a marvellous canvas a crop field makes for such creations. The impact can be absolutely sensational. From the air this formation presented to me a confusing set of impressions and thoughts emphasised by its position on the steeply sloping hillside, almost as if it were an offering of some kind. I wonder what impression is created in your mind? I would like you to try something. Position the picture so the semi-rings are at the bottom of the pictogram and see what comes into your mind. Make a note of this. Now reverse the photograph so the semi-rings are at the top. What are your thoughts now?

PAT DELGADO

EXTON,
1990

I could not resist including this beautiful formation of five circles in such an idyllic setting. Although we have recorded many of these quintuplets in the past, this one seemed special.

The large satellite circles give it a boldness that stamps its authority into the wheat field. The clockwise-swirled central circle measuring 20 metres in diameter with its attendant 6-metre-diameter circles all swirled anti-clockwise is the first instance of this particular combination that has been recorded.

PAT DELGADO

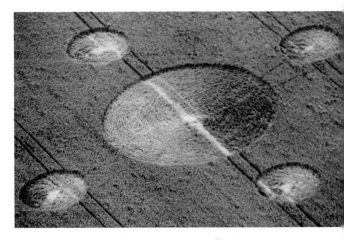

HAZELEY FARM FIELDS,
1990

At the beginning of the first week of June I arrived at the top of Cheesefoot Head hill and stopped in the parking space. My eyes were immediately drawn to a patch of dark marks in a field about half a kilometre away. I took out my binoculars, always an essential part of the kit, and focusing on the marks I could see two circles and a joining pathway. What I could not see plainly was an inexplicable mark to one side of the nearest circle.

The farmer, Gerald James, who had had crop circles on his land in past years which we did not know about, was very interested but

could offer no explanation for this new addition.

It was a long walk along a public footpath to reach this site and a convenient tractor-wheel track took me and my daughter Jan into one of the two immediately apparent circles. I could see both were connected by a slightly curved flattened pathway. Walking out of the clockwise-swirled first circle along this pathway, I was amazed at seeing two curved finger-like troughs on either side of the central path. One end of the troughs entered a ring surrounding the second circle, also clockwise swirled. The flattened crop forming the trough floors was flattened towards and into the ring. There were sweeping overlays of conflicting swathes where crop stems from the troughs and ring intertwined. The artistry was superb.

One very prominent feature was the exaggerated example of gap-seeking that has been mentioned previously in *Circular Evidence*. The tractor-wheel tracks had obviously influenced the inducing energy to depart from its anti-clockwise concentric path. Part of the energy had followed the first wheel track and the other part of the energy had been thrown out into the second wheel track. It had followed this track for a short distance and then recovered, enabling it to complete its

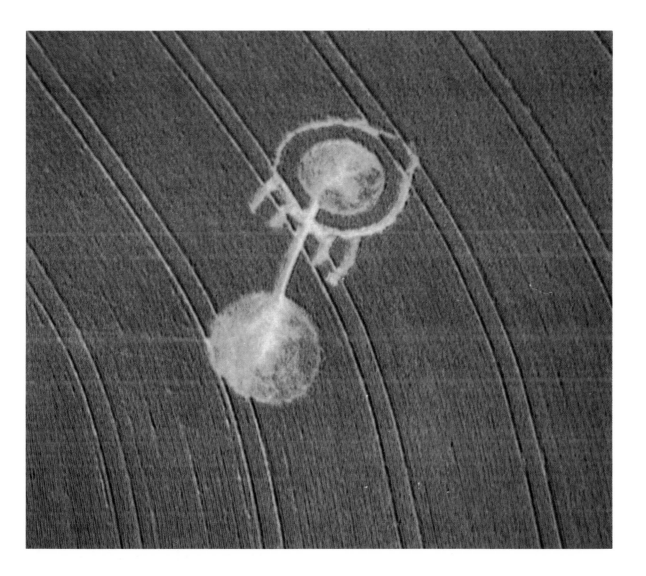

concentric path. It displays a beak-like app-earance from the air and the four 'fingers' have a similarity to jellyfish or octopus tentacles.

When this pictogram is viewed so the 'beak' is on the left and appears to be drooping, it displays a sad quality, as though something has been hurt. Perhaps what it portrays has been injured or partially des-troyed; I am sure that is one of the main intentions.

PAT DELGADO

LICHFIELD, 1990

A friend whom I have known for a few years now and who is a keen crop-formation observer, Bob Skinner, telephoned me early on the morning of Sunday 24 June. He reported that late the previous day he had come across another pictogram. From his description it was different to the others we had visited and this boosted my desire to drive out to the site as soon as possible. Jan came with me, sharing my enthusiasm, and after about half an hour's drive we saw the pictogram. It was near the A34 road at Lichfield and well placed on an elevated position, the sloping ground facing the road.

What we saw confirmed immediately Bob's description of two semi-rings and four troughs. As we have an arrangement with the landowner, I decided to inspect the formation at close quarters after I had taken some photographs from the roadside.

It is always something special entering a new formation for the first time and this was no exception. The lower larger circle was 11 metres in diameter and swirled clockwise. The central pathway was 18 metres long, 1·8 metres wide and swept up the slope. The upper circle was approximately 7 metres across and also clockwise swirled. The inner semi-ring was 1 metre wide and laid clockwise.

The outer semi-ring was the same width but laid anti-clockwise. This semi-ring had a central thin line of standing crop all the way round its length, so it became a twin semi-circular path. The four troughs were 3 metres long and 1·3 metres wide. The floor of each was swept up towards the semi-rings.

From the air, this formation portrayed quietness and serenity, perhaps similar to a symbolistic message carved on a slab of sandstone.

PAT DELGADO

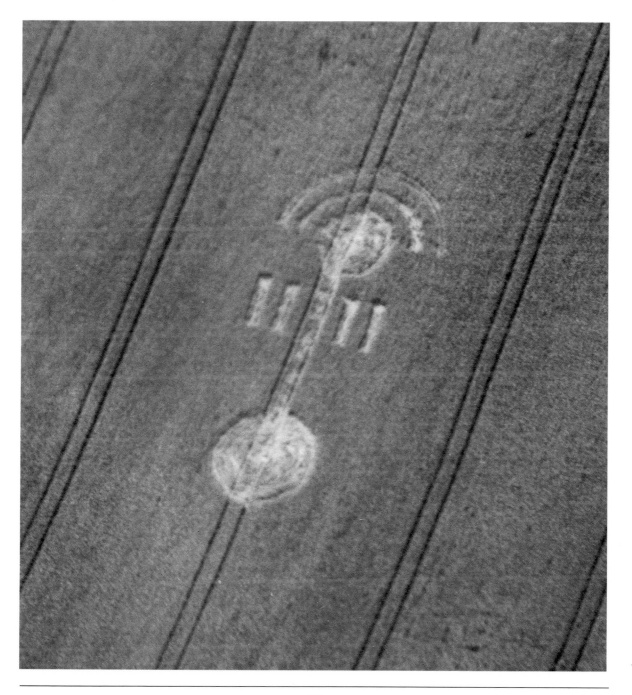

MORESTEAD, 1990

On Saturday 30 June, Angela Green telephoned to report a pictogram next to the Morestead road out of Winchester. On arrival I saw the design was different again to all the others.

The most obvious features were the single troughs either side of the centre path. Closer inspection revealed that the floor of the trough on the left, going up the sloping ground, was laid downhill, while the one on the right was of the opposite direction. Some distortion of the design had taken place, which I saw clearly when I later flew over the site to take aerial photographs.

The pictogram is 31 metres from top to bottom. Both circles are swirled clockwise. The incomplete ring is laid anti-clockwise.

PAT DELGADO

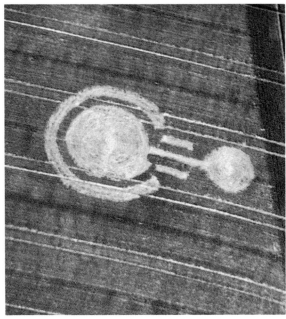

WILTSHIRE CIRCLES,
1990

At 4.00 p.m. on 3 May at Baltic Farm, Bishops Canning, Wiltshire, the farmer, David Shepherd, discovered a large circle stamped into his young wheat field.

Pat and I arrived the following day and found Mr Shepherd intensely interested in knowing more about these large and precise marks which he had seen around his farm for the past four years, but never before that. He questioned us extensively about what we thought could be causing them and then took us to a very remote location where this 23·5-metre clockwise circle could be seen. The site was one of pure beauty, with a Bronze Age enclosure in the field to the northwest, a row of ancient burial mounds (tumuli) to the north and northeast and the amazing earthworks called Wansdyke winding across the western landscape. A Roman road carved through the southern boundary of the field.

Within six weeks the patterns arriving in Wiltshire were of the Celtic Cross type, while a chain of reports in Hampshire revealed an astounding new pictogram family of patterns. No longer could we refer only to mystery circles: we were now seeing rectangles as well as spurs.

On 1 June a television crew from Fuji, Japan, one of many arriving from around the world, were interviewing me in the research office in Andover when I received a most important telephone call. It was from Terry Butcher, the agricultural planning manager of a food company near Devizes, Wiltshire. The hatchery manager, Jim Stirton, had seen a mysterious group of circles with narrow rings around them in a barley field near the golf course at Blackland. It was indeed a crucial call because when Pat and I visited the site the next day the farm foreman, Andrew Woolley, told us that he had found at least twenty other circles on his farm.

During the last two years there has been an increasing number of small circles, between 1 and 5 metres in diameter, scattered around the area where larger and more complex patterns are situated. Most of the new arrivals in this area are of the small randomly-scattered variety. Many can be seen in the photograph. This field contains the largest circle ever seen.

Pat remained in the field with the farm foreman and gathering numbers of the general public while I returned to arrange an aircraft. Local pilot Derek Christopher was banking the aircraft over to our right, aligning it for a route to the west of the new Celtic Cross variety, when he noticed a huge circle about

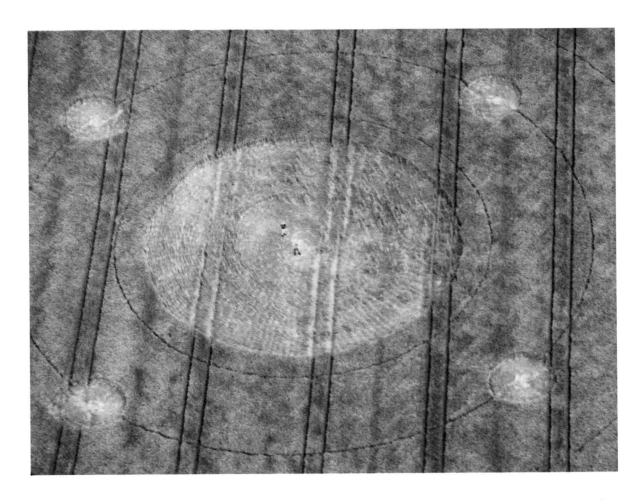

half a mile southwest of the circle in which Pat could still be seen measuring. As many as thirty-six smaller circles were spotted over the whole field. Three major formations were photographed within sight of one another, with over fifty single circles punched into the fields around. The flight was one I will always remember.

The largest circle when measured proved to be over 200 feet (60·9 metres) in diameter with four narrow annular rings encompassing it, the whole being over 300 feet across. Enquiries revealed it was several weeks old and when first found had had only three annular rings. This was a point I put to meteorologist Dr Terence Meaden at a conference on the circles held in Oxford in July. He became highly embarrassed and blatantly personal when words failed him in front of a packed assembly of scientists and media rep-

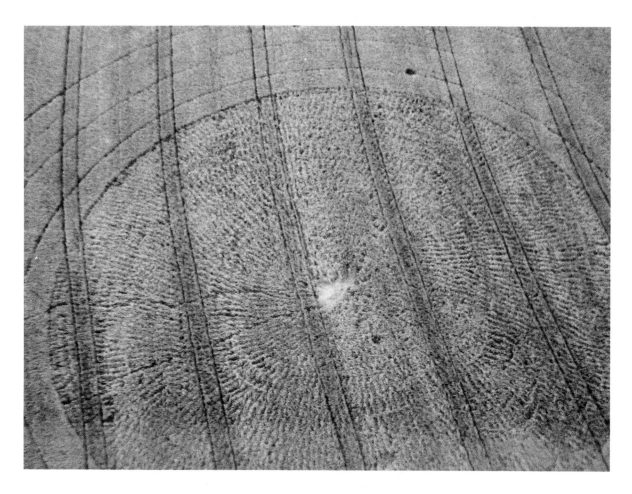

resentatives from many countries. They had come to listen to Dr Meaden's claim that he had solved the mystery, concluding that stationary whirlwinds were responsible as they produced electrically charged vortices, called the plasma vortex, an effect due to certain weather conditions close to hills. I appeared to agitate him further by asking how he accounted for the new pictogram formation in terms of the law of angular momentum, a law of physics which must be complied with for his plasma vortex theory to be credible. He refused to reply. Finally, when I asked why he had not informed the conference of other important questions associated with re-visits to existing formations, it became clear that this British weatherman had been, as it were, undressed on stage. The whirlwind explanation was now seriously ill.

When plant sample analyses were carried

out at my request by laboratories near Stroud, Gloucester, the theory finally died. I

Plant crystals under microscope.

Above: Control sample.

Below: From inside circle – a dramatic change.

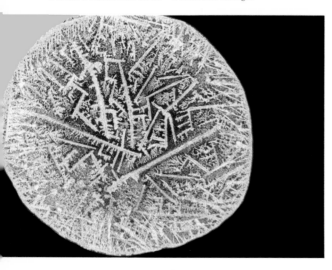

asked Rosemary and Kenneth Spelman to carry out a special process on the plant samples taken from the circles Terry Butcher had reported. Rosemary and Kenneth own the only laboratories in the UK conducting such a test and the results were exciting. As the photographs show, the energy pattern of the crystals produced by a distillation process from the plants inside the circles was dramatically different to that from control samples taken from plants in the same field.

With all this new evidence we knew that we were looking at a very real and important phenomenon which had nothing to do with hoaxing, helicopters or whirlwinds. But what was causing such incredibly beautiful patterns?

As more circles arrived in this small corner of Wiltshire, four miles away at Beckhampton, where the 'noise' had been recorded by national television, new circles had appeared, but so far these were only small and relatively unexciting. It was some weeks later that the farm foreman at Blackland, Andrew Woolley, remembered to tell me that his shepherd had mentioned to him the difficulties he had had with four of his dogs on the same night the Celtic Cross circle arrived. The behaviour of his dogs was most unusual; they barked relentlessly during the night and would not settle on command which was totally out of character.

During the closing weeks of the summer season, Pat and I planned Operation Blackbird, an international surveillance operation in this country, with the involvement of British, American, German, Japanese and French personnel.   COLIN ANDREWS

LONGWOOD ESTATE, 1990

This was one of the largest formations we had seen until the appearance of the well publicised pictogram at Alton Barnes in the Vale of Pewsey, Wiltshire, pictured and described further on. This one, at Longwood Estate, measured nearly 50 metres in length and was yet another permutation of circles, rings, troughs and pathways.

The wide ring surrounding the upper circle accentuates its size. Both the circles and the ring are flattened and swirled clockwise. Although this formation is nearly 400 metres from the road, it is very readily viewed from there and is very attractive because of its size and symmetry. Its obliquely sloping position is enigmatic in itself.

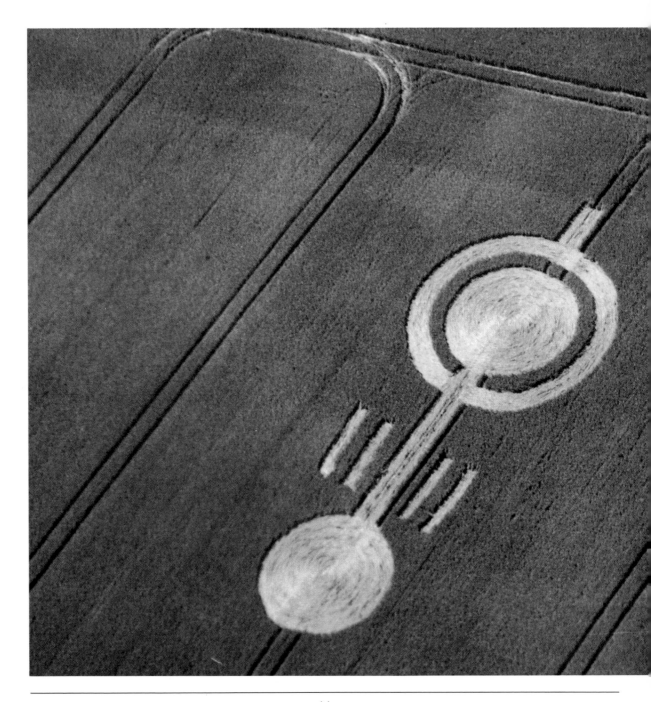

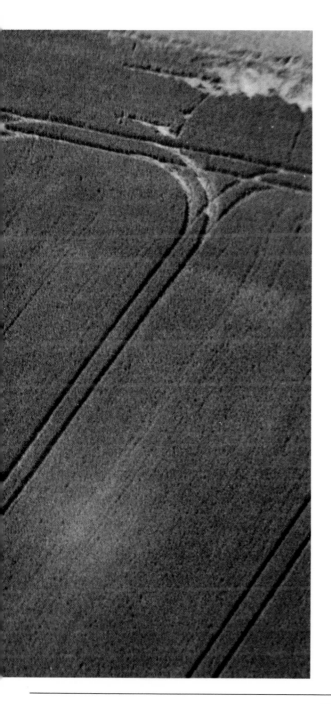

The width of the ring is 2 metres and it is almost perfectly circular with a slight flattening of the circle and ring on the right-hand side. This flattening has been noticed on other circles and rings over the years and it seems to occur quite randomly and cannot be associated with any crop differences.

Yet another anomaly lies in the floors of the troughs. The top ends of the two inner troughs have orange patches, which are the bottom of the stems and bare earth. This means the crop is flattened away from that end. The two outer troughs are flattened in the opposite direction but the camera angle hides the little patch behind the standing crop at the bottom end. Mysteries upon mysteries – why is there a contraflow of troughs?

What looks like a continuation of the central path projecting beyond the top of the ring is actually swathed in the opposite direction to the connecting pathway. Speculation has no part to play in this book, but . . . could this short path have been on its way to a third circle?

The central pathway is not positioned centrally over the tractor-wheel tracks. It runs off-line by about 1·3 metres as can be seen where the short path terminates. On the right-hand side of both pathways is a thin 15-cm-wide line of standing crop, a very fine detail indeed which shows the precise alignment capability of whatever is controlling the creative energy.

This evolving phenomenon is certainly producing some spectacular designs in the crop fields.

Pat Delgado

CHEESEFOOT HEAD, *1986*

In the light of the appearance of so many new and complex formations in 1990, an incident that had occurred back in 1986 now seemed to take on an extra significance. Little had we known what a wonderful surprise was in store for us that day. It was during the second week in August that we had received a report that a circle had appeared in a field south of the Punch Bowl, a natural amphitheatre at Cheesefoot Head, near Winchester. Busty Taylor was to fly Jan and myself to the area of the report so we could pinpoint the actual locality. We found it with no problem and took a number of photographs. On the return journey it was suggested we fly over the Punch Bowl to see whether there were any additional circles and rings of which we were presently unaware.

As is usual on these occasions our three pairs of eyes were constantly scanning the fields below. There is almost a competitive atmosphere, as though there were a prize for the first person to spot a new circle.

As we approached the Punch Bowl we could see the known circles in their respective positions but when we were almost over the boundary fence, we shouted, almost in unison, 'What is that?' Below us was a line of letters making up what seemed to be one long word. I

could not understand it at first but I quickly focused my camera on the writing and took several shots as Busty circled the area. I must say Busty did very well to hold the plane on a steady run, such was the shock and excitement at this most unexpected sight. Staring at the letters we tried to pronounce the word and as we began our departure from over it, it dawned on us that it was four words joined together. So instead of WEARENOTALONE it was WE ARE NOT ALONE. (But not quite: can you see anything peculiar about the N in ALONE?)

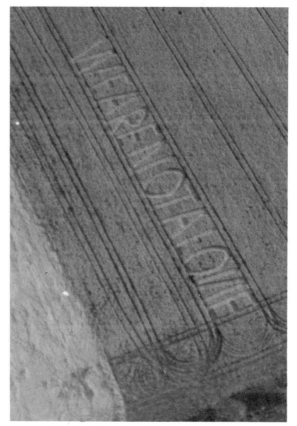

When we had landed I decided to drive immediately back to the Punch Bowl to take some ground shots. It was just as well I did because as I descended the steep side of the natural depression I was very impressed with the size of the creation lying before me.

Taking my photographs I was aware of a machine of some kind approaching from the direction of the farm buildings. Unfortunately, as it turned out, I had to leave for an important appointment but when I returned to the Punch Bowl an hour later, I found the reason for the machine. It was a harvesting machine and it had removed all the letters as can be seen in the photograph.

When I spoke to the farmer a few days later it became apparent why he had done this. He explained he had driven round the field late the previous evening and the letters were not there. Very early the next morning one of his men reported what he had seen and he had verified it himself. As soon as he was able to organise a machine to remove the evidence, he had done so, but not before I was able to record it. I asked for his views about the letters and he had simply no explanation and was utterly astounded. It was a massive configuration created at night. Nobody reported seeing anything that evening or during the night of its arrival and nobody has claimed to have hoaxed it.

Each letter was 36·5 metres from top to bottom and the whole word was 183 metres long. Each letter was flattened in the same manner as we are now seeing in the rings and pathways of the pictograms.

No doubt the sceptics will draw their own conclusions and there will also be people who claim to be the originators, but there are some questions waiting to be answered concerning known pertinent details not printed here.

Was the statement in the field connected with what we are seeing today?

PAT DELGADO

ALTON BARNES, 1990

When the news of a truly astounding crop formation reached us, it was with even more anticipation than usual that we quickly made our way to Pewsey Downs in Wiltshire. After parking our cars we walked up the ridge and soon were looking down into a field containing the most amazing pictogram we had ever seen. As can be seen from the photograph, a detailed description would almost take a whole book, so complicated is the pattern.

We took some pictures and then went into the field, with the permission of Mr Carson, the farmer. There was so much to study in the complex shapes, especially the claw- or key-like features. The circular areas were precise and well defined. Their centres presented classic tight spirals and the edges were sharp. The central pathways were laid straight and undamaged as were all the other floor areas. The key-like forms were of special interest because of the square and rectangular shapes that dominated the whole design. Such a dramatic departure from even the pictograms of recent weeks was quite breathtaking, and the escalation of presentation seemed quite unreal. It may be important to note that residents of Alton Priors and Alton Barnes reported a sudden outburst of dogs' barking at 2.20 a.m. on the morning these pictograms were discovered.

The floor lays of the key features gave the impression of a deliberate attempt to show what could be achieved in presenting shapes removed from any circular motion.

The two long formations look similar but certain details are different. The separate single circle and key feature is just as difficult to understand as the extended complexes.

This popular formation has been visited by several thousand people; the farmer who owns this field started charging an entry fee. Sadly, this site suffered dreadful disfigurement by visitors who pounded a central pathway through the whole length of the pattern, ruining the original design.

PAT DELGADO

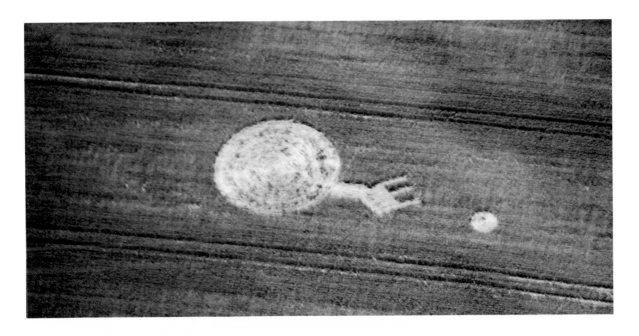

BECKHAMPTON,
1990

It was the telephone call from farmer Stephen Horton of Firs Farm, Beckhampton in Wiltshire that provoked a new wave of wonder about crop formations. The call came one morning while I was busy at Operation Black-bird, the international surveillance at Bratton in Wiltshire. He said he had found some most peculiar shapes flattened into one of his wheat fields and he suggested Colin and I go over to see him as soon as possible. Matthew

Lawrence, one of our operators at the surveillance site, came too. We met up with Colin at the farm and then Stephen was ready to show us the position of the formations. He asked us if we would like to see them from a high position first and we agreed.

It was an amazing sight. In the foreground we could see a wide 'S' swirl joining up three circles, but the 'S' shape was reversed. Beyond this we could make out two dark patches in the carpet of wheat where the other two formations were. Anticipation was high.

The same old excitement, with adrenalin flowing, was present as I approached the first circle. This was 14 metres in diameter and anti-clockwise swirled, beautifully laid down but with slight corrugations around the sharp edges.

Unfortunately, it is imperative to fly over these formations to take photographs as soon as possible after they have been created because of the damage caused by thoughtless visitors. This damage is shown clearly by the six breaches into the large circle on the right.

The pristine beauty of the floor lays was highlighted by sun reflection making it easy to imagine the patterning process in action. Starting at the large circle, it flows into the

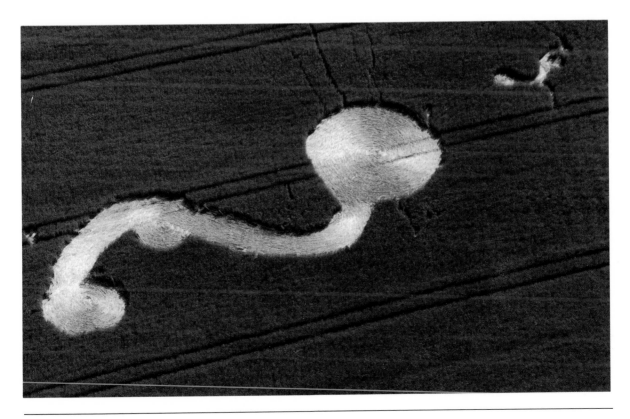

4-metre-wide pathway which gently curves round into the second circle. Something very clever occurs here; if you study the second circle lay, the path flow coming in from the right appears to curl round to complete the circle before it slides under the entry path and exits on the left-hand side. From there the curve of the path changes direction to the right and terminates by forming a third circle of anti-clockwise rotation. The central swirl of the circle was a work of art. Individual plant stems were splayed out in a fan shape round the base of an upward-swathed central feature.

The energies I sensed in this formation were very strong. There seems to be an amplifying effect where circles are joined by pathways and with these curved pathways it was as if extra momentum was gained. This was not the time, however, to read all the energies present – but I had discovered enough to know they existed in powerful complexity.

Matthew and I spent some time taking photographs at eye level and from the top of his camera pole, which thoughtfully he had brought along. The formation was very photogenic and I was tempted to take many pictures. The small feature on the right of the photograph is a spoiled delicate feature which was a 3-metre circle with a tail coming away from it which flowed into a 1·5-metre circle as

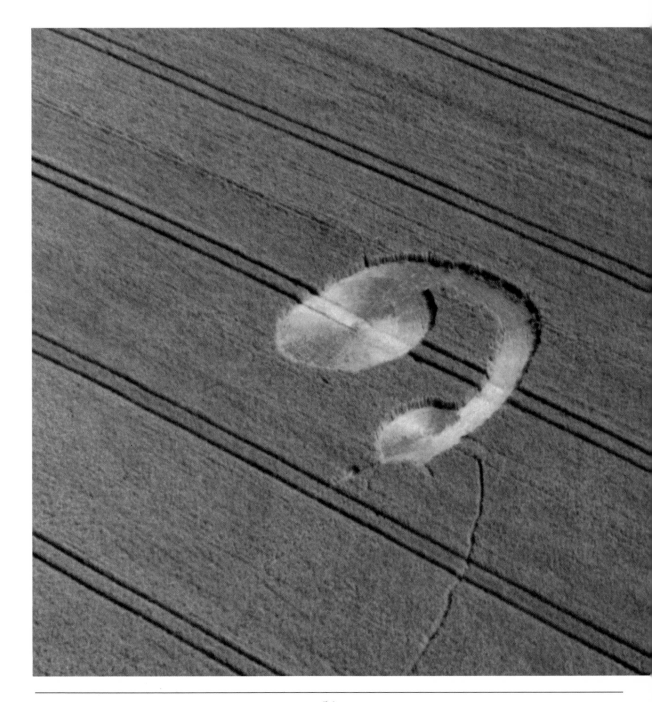

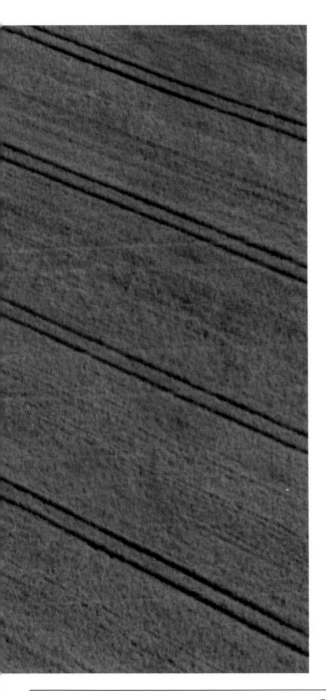

well as continuing on into a 1-metre circle. This formation was almost a miniature of the large one but with opposite shaped curves.

We moved on across the field and came abreast of the most stunning shape of all, the triangle. Over the years we have said many times that it would be the ultimate display if a triangle were created, and here it was. I felt as though a milestone had been reached. There was a bonus to come, too, for on either side of the triangle were the now familiar box-like features, a pair on each side. I could hardly believe my eyes when I realised one of the features of each pair was a 3-metre-long wedge-shaped triangle, with a 1-metre-wide base. At last, I had confirmation of something that has been on my mind for four years: any shape is possible if the patterns are formed with brush-like strokes of energy.

The main triangle dimensions were 9·5 metres at the base with each side 14 metres long. The main area of the triangle was filled with a clockwise-swirled circle from which this swirl was carried outwards to each corner.

To reach the next formation we had to walk out of the field, along the edge of it and up another set of tractor-wheel tracks. This brought us into the beautiful headphone-shaped pattern with its clockwise-swirled circle measuring 14 metres across. Leading from this a 4-metre-wide pathway struck out and curved round to the right for about 180 degrees. It entered tangentially a 7-metre circle, also swirled clockwise. This circle contained a striking tightly-wound central vase-like structure. It would have been a credit to any ornamental garden.

PAT DELGADO

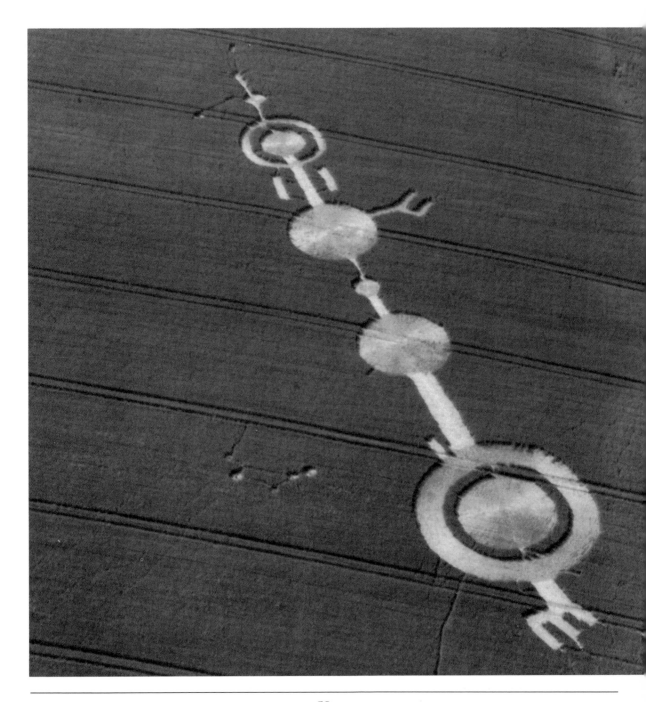

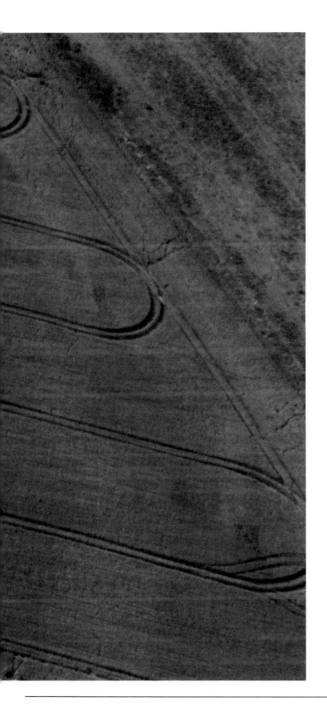

ALLINGTON DOWN,
1990

The weather was hot and dry with drought conditions beginning to cause widespread concern. Farmers were using all their resources to cut their fields as quickly as possible because the cereal crops were ripening faster than they could be harvested.

An unwelcome interruption to the highly organised harvesting at Allington Down was the discovery by the farmer, David Reid, early one morning in late July, of the most incredible sight he could have imagined. Strung across his field was a sight one could picture only in a dream. Four circles, two with rings, were linked by pathways formed along a straight line. From where he stood, on a track running through his farm, the formation stretched nearly 200 metres over and beyond the top of the brow. David Reid had received visits from the mystery source on several occasions during the previous two years, but this was much more spectacular and, interestingly, in a different field.

He is a very down-to-earth man and not at all prone to fanciful ideas, but this left him virtually speechless. He decided to follow the idea of nearby farmer Tim Carson, who had set up a caravan at the edge of a field in which a similar set of marks had appeared and was charging £1 per person for entry into his field.

David Reid could see the merit of recovering the costs of further damage to his crop by the growing tidal wave of people tramping across the field to view these amazing graphic designs.

Pat and I met him at the entrance to a temporary car park – a grass meadow – close to the multiple pictogram. It was already three-quarters full with more visitors arriving by the minute. He commented, 'It was not there when I drove down here last evening, but appeared here during the night. I cannot think of anything that could do this, can you?' He looked into our eyes with a desperate hopefulness that we might put his mind at rest. We could not.

This astounding array of circles, rings, fingers and boxes, each one positioned in obvious association with its neighbours, combined to form a feature resembling a highly decorated Indian totem pole.

This new family of crop markings made the simple single circles that were appearing elsewhere seem somewhat insignificant. The sheer graphic design, so pictorial, symbolic and distinct, created visions of a cosmic finger drawing pictures in the fields of southern England. Each blade of wheat was positioned with such precision and respect for its neighbours, and with such care as to leave each plant bent to the ground but undamaged.

Hundreds of people were telephoning and writing letters to us stating the now obvious fact that nothing in nature could have these effects. They were troubled too by the Government's view that stationary whirlwinds were responsible. What Pat and I were looking at here must once and for all remove any possibility of that theory's being remotely credible.

We noticed that the major axis of the pictogram pointed directly at nearby Silbury Hill, and straddled the tractor tramlines at an angle of about 45 degrees. The other two discoveries, which contained similar markings, had been found running parallel to those tyre marks, while also close by in the same field were several small buckshot circles; however, these were remote from the tramlines and appeared to be randomly positioned. How much more complex could this phenomenon become? We both share the view: YOU HAVE NOT SEEN ANYTHING YET!

COLIN ANDREWS

FARLEY MOUNT,
1990

I sped to a location known as Farley Mount following several reports from various crop watchers. The monument, placed on an ancient Bronze Age barrow to commemorate the exploit of a certain horse and rider, is in the centre of a circular grassed patch. To the south of this area the ground drops away, so it was not immediately obvious that a very striking circle with a huge surrounding ring had appeared.

It was difficult to see just how large it was from ground level and this is where the camera pole came in useful. Elevation and a wide-angle lens on the camera have captured many outstanding views of crop formations.

The 8-metre circle was swirled clockwise and surrounded by a 45-metre anti-clockwise-

swirled ring. The ring width varied from 3 to 4 metres with some gap-seeking where it traversed the tractor-wheel tracks.

PAT DELGADO

PEPPERBOX HILL,
1990

The appearance of the smaller formation occurred four days after the larger one. Rick Howell, a pilot and good friend of mine, secured these excellent photographs for me.

The three circles and the ring of the larger formation were all clockwise swirled. The pathway to the small circle on the left was laid in the opposite direction to that passing through the centre of the ring. The large circle and ring were approximately 15 metres in diameter, the lesser circle was 10 metres and the small circle was 5 metres. The two

rectangular boxes were 7 metres long and 1 metre wide. One peculiar feature was the 1·5-metre offset position of the ring to its traversing pathway.

The smaller formation had circles of 14 and 12 metres in diameter, both swirled clockwise. The triple connecting pathway is once again unique.

None of these pictograms is the same as any other. It is as though all the pieces are in a box and they can be fitted together in various ways. The details of these two formations were kindly supplied by Alan Doel, one of the many dedicated crop watchers who are so generous with their time.

PAT DELGADO

ETCHILHAMPTON, 1990

With the assistance of Pat I co-ordinated an intensive surveillance called Operation Blackbird at the Westbury White Horse for three weeks during July 1990. Many complex cameras were positioned to monitor anything unusual along a corridor of one mile between the villages of Westbury and Bratton where numerous circles have appeared since 1980. We had received the highest level of assistance and co-operation from the British Army and private companies, including the BBC, Nippon Television, Civil Defence Supply, Cloud 9 Limited and Envin Scientific Products. We were involved in over 130 television and radio interviews as well as participating in two film documentaries. However, more will be written about Operation Blackbird at a later date.

Early one morning while we were at the surveillance control caravan we received a report from the crew of an army helicopter of a windmill-shaped design at Etchilhampton, approximately 1·5 miles southeast of Devizes. Once again a new type of pictogram had formed in a field of golden-brown cereal which was below an ancient hill fort.

Because we had a great deal of technical equipment and personnel at the surveillance site, this was to date the best opportunity to investigate some of the fringe reports associated with some of the circles. We held an urgent meeting at the Blackbird camp and decided to mobilise experts from the engineering department of the BBC based in London and the surveillance unit of Cloud 9 Limited.

A convoy of vehicles set out towards Etchilhampton, led by Pat and myself. We drove off the main highway and up a very rough track for some distance, reaching the field a few minutes later. The moment we came to a standstill Pat and I entered the field with the usual impatient enthusiasm while the engineers set up the specialised equipment. As we approached the formation we looked back towards the track and could see Cloud 9's large hydraulic mast with a videocamera attached climbing high into the sky; more aerials were being assembled on top of the other vehicles nearby. Within minutes of our arrival an army helicopter arrived uninvited and hovered over the pictogram within a few feet of us – it seemed at one moment that the pilot might actually land the craft in the crop, he was so close.

The link spurs striking out from the outer ring were flattened in an outward direction, while the opposing spurs were flattened inwards. The two rings and large circles were spiralled. This was a very heavily flattened formation where not a single plant was left standing.

Of the many tests carried out only one showed encouraging results. An electrostatic-detection device revealed an unusual fluctuation in one part of the flattened crop. A most strange event was about to happen.

We had completed another heavy schedule of television work and it was a day of record high temperatures. That evening after we had all left for home, Mike Carrie, a director of Cloud 9 who had set up his equipment to monitor anything that moved in the formation that night, decided to walk into the circle and take a closer look. He soon wished he had not.

While standing in the area of the single ring, he bent over to look into a soil recess and was greeted by a loud noise around his head. He later told us that from his technical experience he recognised how powerful the energy must have been that was responsible. 'You just know,' he said. I asked, 'How far away was it from you? Did you see anything?' Mike replied, 'Nothing could be seen, but whatever caused it was right around my head, just inches away.'

The noise he described was the same as I experienced during the BBC filming incident at Beckhampton that I described earlier, as well as in an event at Kimpton in Hampshire, described on page 66 of *Circular Evidence*.

COLIN ANDREWS

WESTBURY, 1990

An interesting report was made to us concerning a keen crop watcher. He had been observing a certain field for a number of days because he had a feeling a crop-formation event would occur there.

During one afternoon he was puzzled by an awareness that the angle of the shadow thrown on to the field by one group of trees appeared to be quite different to the shadow angle of a group of trees a little further away. He actually walked to check this from both groups of trees and confirmed this peculiar anomaly. He checked his watch at the second position and found he had lost half an hour.

Now even more puzzled he returned to the original position and discovered he had regained what he judged to be normal time again. The following morning he returned to the same location and discovered a circle with three satellites had been created. His account of the events was given with calm, almost embarrassed sincerity.

A few days later while flying in that area, Rick Howell saw that group of circles and managed to secure the accompanying photograph.

PAT DELGADO

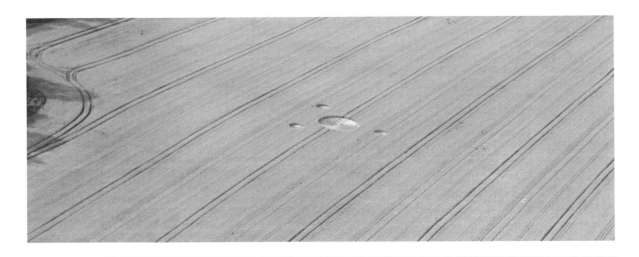

HAZELEY FARM FIELDS,
1990

This is surely one of the most distinguished formations we have been privileged to visit. The absolute beauty and symmetrical position of the pattern is a joy to see.

The sweep of the swirls and the soft straight lays of the pathways were of such elegance it gave me the feeling of wanting to remain there for several hours.

Unfortunately, other commitments were pressing and I had to make the most of the short time I could stay. However, I did have enough time to discover a hole in the soil,

which was about 2 metres from the centre of the circle at the right-hand side of the photograph. This hole puzzled me. It went down at an angle of 45 degrees and its depth was more than the 30-cm length of straw I pushed down it. There was a small amount of loose soil around the top of the hole but definitely far too little to account for what must have been removed.

The overlapping of the pathway lays where they entered the circles was what could be termed straw perfect. Here was yet another mysterious, artistic delight.

PAT DELGADO

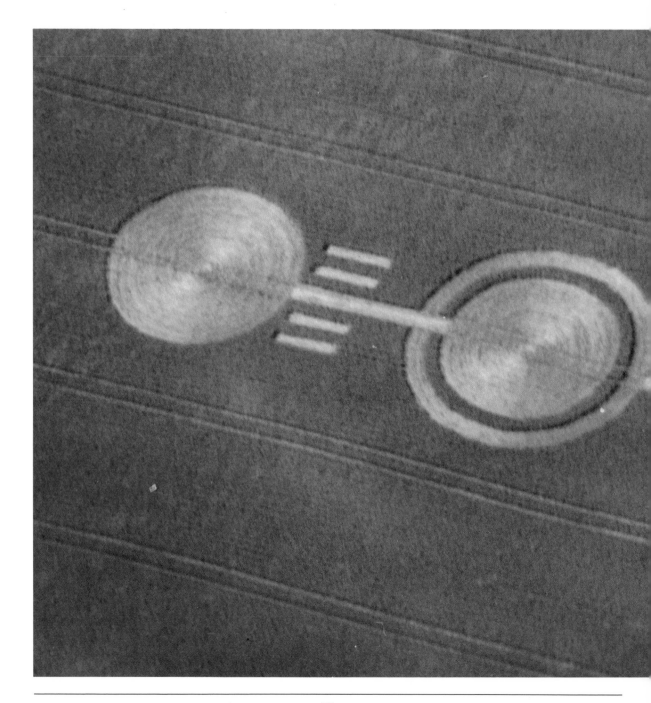

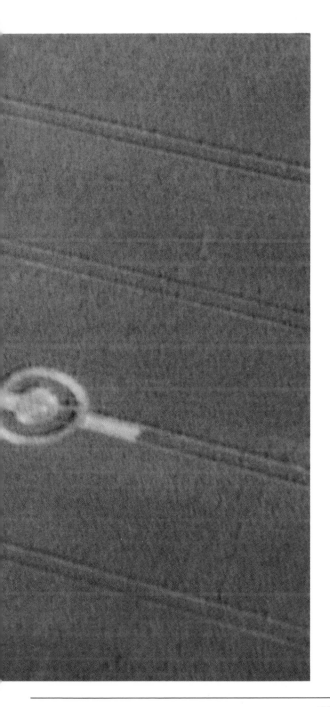

CRAWLEY DOWNS, *1990*

Colin's father, Gordon Andrews, while driving to meet Colin at a filming session, passed these circles in a field near the road. When he reported to us what he had seen, we were very interested, and on our way back home we stopped to investigate. There before us was yet another splendid and fascinating formation, consisting of three clockwise-swirled circles, two with outer rings, and a central pathway (laid from right to left as you look at the photograph) flanked by two pairs of rectangular troughs. The troughs measured 4 metres by 1.5 metres. The breaks in the pathway where it entered the first two circles were an unusual feature. We were truly learning never to know what to expect next.

PAT DELGADO

CROP-FORMATION PATTERNS

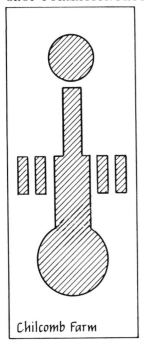

Chilcomb Farm

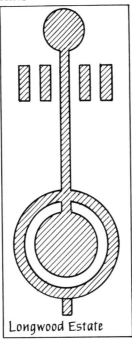

Longwood Estate

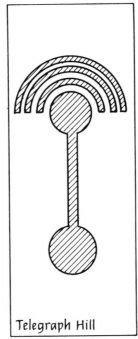

Telegraph Hill

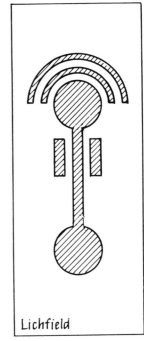

Lichfield

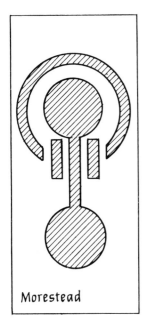

Morestead

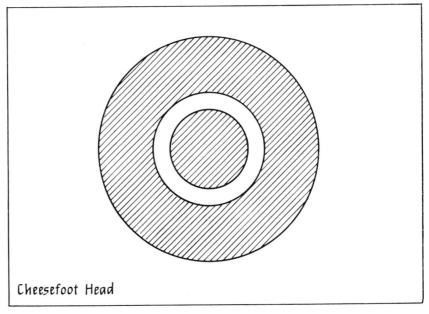

Cheesefoot Head

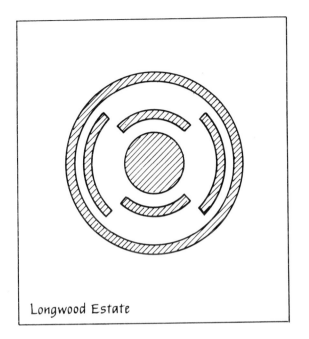

Longwood Estate

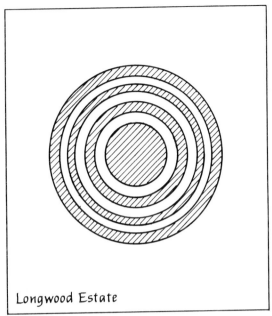

Longwood Estate

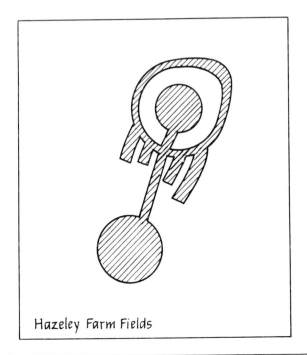

Hazeley Farm Fields

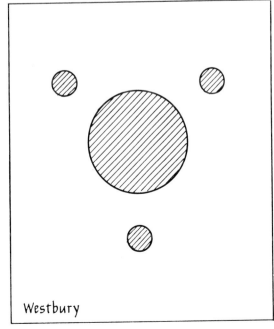

Westbury

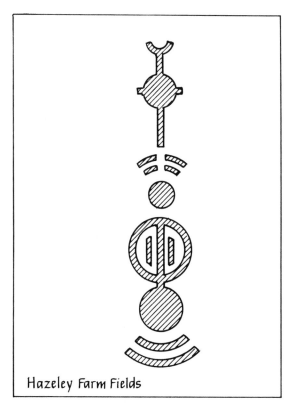

Hazeley Farm Fields

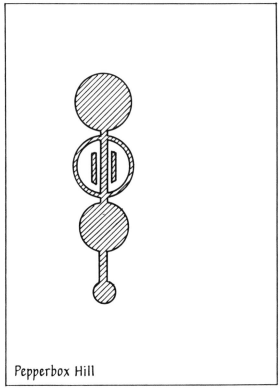

Pepperbox Hill

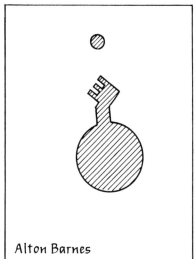

Alton Barnes

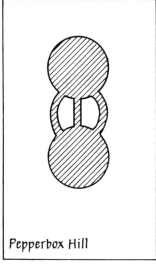

Pepperbox Hill

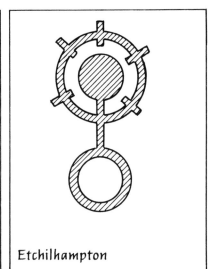

Etchilhampton

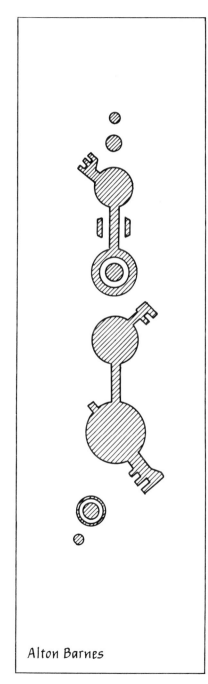

Alton Barnes

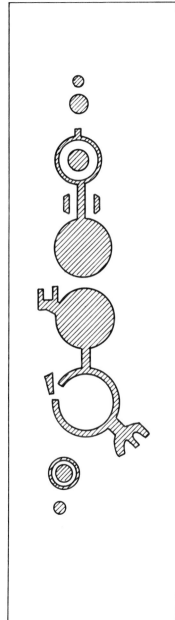

Alton Barnes

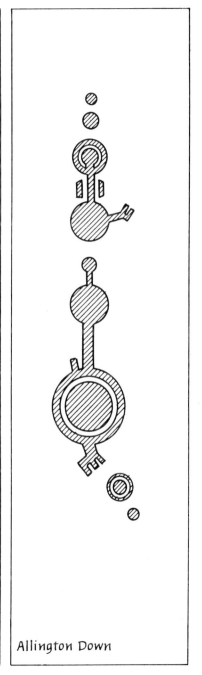

Allington Down

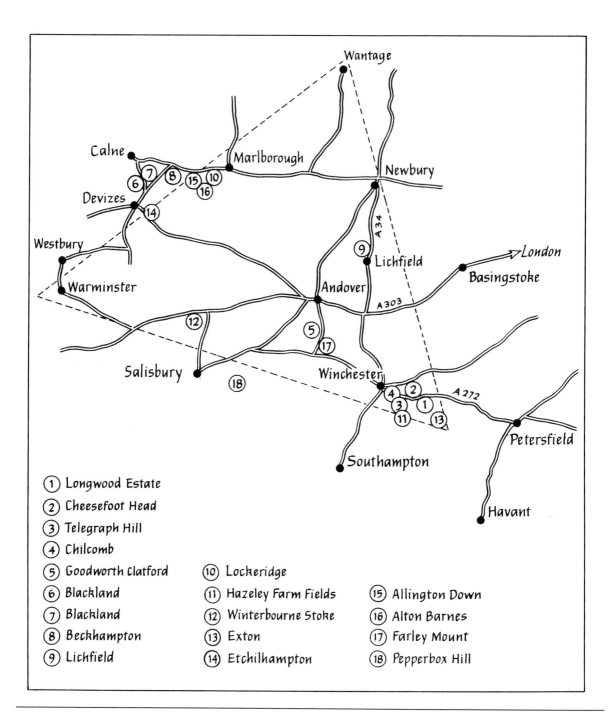

① Longwood Estate
② Cheesefoot Head
③ Telegraph Hill
④ Chilcomb
⑤ Goodworth Clatford
⑥ Blackland
⑦ Blackland
⑧ Beckhampton
⑨ Lichfield
⑩ Lockeridge
⑪ Hazeley Farm Fields
⑫ Winterbourne Stoke
⑬ Exton
⑭ Etchilhampton
⑮ Allington Down
⑯ Alton Barnes
⑰ Farley Mount
⑱ Pepperbox Hill

Theories Update

Since *Circular Evidence* was first published in July 1989, and the resulting media coverage of the subject, the response from readers has been overwhelming. Many people have obviously had a yearning, suppressed until now, to communicate personal experiences, sensations and emotions, highlighting an awareness of something that appears to be another part of our material world.

It is as though orthodox physics and science have been on trial for the last ten years and have failed to produce an answer. The determined search for a solution to the crop-formations mystery is following a path that is slowly eliminating various theories. In addition to the requirements previously laid out, necessary to cover all the conditions found in crop-formations, we must now take into consideration the following: remotely placed rectangular boxes or troughs where floors are laid straight and flat, and some of which contain a contraflow of flattened crop; long straight pathways connecting two circles; and semi-circular ring pathways, some of which have adjacent ones flattened in opposite directions.

At present we are seeing formations created with permutations of circles, semi-circular ring paths, rings, parts of rings, rectangular troughs, long straight pathways, contra-rotation and contraflows. With these ingredients it should be possible to create just about any design. No doubt we will see far more than have been displayed so far. Even at the time of going to press, new formations are appearing.

Here is a list of theories and suggestions that have been offered during the first half of 1990. The effects of underground water. Magnetic fields. Space energy. Farm machinery wheel tracks. Crop virus. Insects. Birds. Extraterrestial beings. UFOs. Chemicals. Earthquakes. A type of electrical force. Witchcraft. Biblical connections. Volcanic effects. Earth forces. Energy lines. Ley lines. Radio frequencies. Weather conditions. Vortices. Archaeological effects. Earth satellite effects. Gravity effects. Religious effects. Occult effects. Spiritual effects. Ultrasonics. Effects of the planets. Effects from space programme debris. Electromagnetism.

So, it can be seen, the suggestions are increasing. Each does not represent the opinion of one person alone. Many people can be listed under each heading.

The new complex pictograms have announced the arrival of the next phase in the display of this phenomenon.

My original statement that not all that is seen is what it seems to be has been completely substantiated. It is as though the straight pathway, the straight troughs and the partial rings contained in the pictograms are created deliberately to eliminate all vortex-based theories. It will encourage the narrow-minded to accept there is endless knowledge to be gained beyond the pigeon-holing attitude of conventional science. It must be accepted that there are energies that we do not understand.

When collating the suggestions it was interesting to note the two longest lists came under electromagnetism and spiritual effects. This may have arisen because it is well known that the effect of electromagnetism is used to a great extent to help us in today's world. Equally, spiritual effects can be seen as an answer to so many mysterious occurrences – the hand of God, to use a well-known phrase. I am sure all will be explained at some time in the future. Maybe some of us know the answer already. So much of what we are familiar with today was not even dreamed of only a hundred years ago.

How and when will we become aware of how and why crop formations are created? I have been asked many times what my personal thoughts are on how these formations are created. People who know me will tell you I am not an egotistical man and have no wish to sensationalise or create an air of mystery. I can only relate what has happened to me as being my own evolving perception of the phenomenon. You will have read of my experiences at Beckhampton in 1989. But I first recognised I had an ability for detecting energy when I dowsed tumuli. Dowsing is one of the windows through which many people see a way of at least contacting forces that are not understood. Everyone can dowse to some extent, and those who have experienced even the slightest result will be aware of something else beyond tangibility.

Pendulums and dowsing rods are restrictive mechanical aids to display detected energies and will display a few different energies by certain movements. I soon realised rods were a hindrance to progress in understanding more about the energies surrounding us. During a session dowsing a tumulus, I became aware I was detecting only a tiny fraction of what there was to be discovered. I abandoned the rods and started to use my bare hands. Immediately a whole new world of information opened up. It was the beginning of my really understanding energies and the intelligence that controls them. I became aware that everything has its own energy pattern – buildings, rivers, trees, people, animals, insects and even blades of grass – and that it was universal.

At this point, I understood the connection with the crop-formation creation energies; energies that could be manipulated. This became apparent when I involuntarily passed my hands across a friend's forehead when he complained of a headache. The headache just disappeared and I was channelling energy. Many similar occasions followed. What else could be done with these masses of different energies? Anything, I suppose. Healing, removal of uncomfortable energies from buildings, detecting anything in the ground no matter how deep, detecting energies in the atmosphere – the possibilities are limitless.

The next short step is to be aware that an intelligence can select a certain energy or energies to perform particular functions. Creating crop formations is one of them.

In the light of the present state of stalemate that has been reached with theories, I will describe the basis only of my 'awareness', which became apparent to me in 1988.

I invite you to consider the inducement to move crops or vegetation from their vertical position as a two-part function. The recent departure of the phenomenon from the familiar circular shapes now gives much greater credence to this avenue of understanding. Only the mechanics of the manipulation will be described here. What the energy is and who controls it will be explained at a time considered to be more fitting.

First, a preparatory or priming function takes place in order that each stem is 'programmed' to move in a pre-designated direction. This function, sourced above the ground, is similar to drawing a plan-view design with a pencil. The area to be affected is entirely covered with strokes in the direction each plant stem is intended to be laid or moved. From the floor swathes we have studied in formations, it can be judged that the stroke width inducing the stems can vary from 1 to about 15 centimetres.

Once this phase has been accomplished, the pattern is now waiting, like invisible ink on paper, for the second function. This may be termed the command or trigger function and is sourced below the ground under the primed area. The triggering function is directed upwards when required and when it is, each stem is activated to move to its intended new position in a programmed sequence.

This upward-moving trigger function is responsible for ejecting some plants complete with roots as has been previously recorded. Strength variation of the two functions also explains the variation of crop-flattening. The selection of non-affected stems is explained by the priming function's missing those stems to be left vertical. One crop stem or a whole field can be manipulated if so desired. Any shape or design, including figures and letters, can be displayed in any crop anywhere.

The interval between priming and triggering would also affect how well the crop was laid down owing to plant growth and a slow dissipation of priming energy.

It will be recognised from the description of this special 'awareness' that it is totally dissociated from any form of orthodox physics unless physicists are prepared to admit to similarities of known functions.

PAT DELGADO

CONCLUSIONS

Evolution – therein lie all the answers. It is at work everywhere.

The development of this phenomenon was never more obvious than in the first half of 1990. The incredible designs now appearing in fields, surpassing all subtleties of previous years, are a demonstration of energies and an intelligence beyond the realm of scientific dogma.

The unfolding drama of the crop-formation enigma is a deliberate attempt to expand our awareness. Careful consideration of what is displayed and described here will help to overcome any reluctance to accept that there is much to be learned beyond present orthodox physics.

PAT DELGADO